Shakespeare
THE ANIMATED TALES

THE TAMING OF THE SHREW

ABRIDGED BY LEON GARFIELD

ILLUSTRATED BY OLGA TITOVA

BBC

THE TAMING OF THE SHREW

J822

Shakespeare The Animated Tales is a multinational venture conceived by S4C,
Channel 4 Wales. Produced in Russia, Wales and England, the series has been financed by S4C
and the BBC (UK), Christmas Films (Russia), Home Box Office (USA) and Fujisankei (Japan).

Academic Panel
Professor Stanley Wells
Dr Rex Gibson

Educational Adviser
Michael Marland

Publishing Editor and Co-ordinator
Jane Fior

Book Design
Fiona Macmillan and Ness Wood

Animation Director for *The Taming of the Shrew*
Aida Ziablikova of Christmas Films, Moscow

Series Editors
Martin Lamb and Penelope Middelboe, Right Angle, Tenby, Wales

Executive Producers
Christopher Grace (S4C)
Elizabeth Babakhina (Christmas Films)

Associate Producer
Theresa Plummer Andrews (BBC)

First published in 1994
by William Heinemann Ltd
an imprint of Reed Consumer Books Ltd
Michelin House, 81 Fulham Road, London SW3 6RB
and Auckland, Melbourne, Singapore and Toronto
Copyright © Shakespeare Animated Films/Christmas Films 1994

Printed and bound in the UK by BPC Paulton Books Limited

First Published in 1994
Educational Supplement by Linda Marsh
Educational Supplement © Linda Marsh/BBC Educational Publishing 1994

BBC Educational Publishing
BBC White City, 201 Wood Lane
London W12 7TS

The author's moral rights have been asserted

ISBN 0 563 39742 X

The publishers would like to thank Paul Cox for
the series logo illustration, Carol Kemp for
her calligraphy, and Rosa Fior and Celia Salisbury Jones
for their help on the books.

William Shakespeare

Martin Droeshout sculpsit London.

WILLIAM SHAKESPEARE

NEXT TO GOD, A wise man once said, Shakespeare created most. In the thirty-seven plays that are his chief legacy to the world – and surely no-one ever left a richer! – human nature is displayed in all its astonishing variety.

He has enriched the stage with matchless comedies, tragedies, histories, and, towards the end of his life, with plays that defy all description, strange plays that haunt the imagination like visions.

His range is enormous: kings and queens, priests, princes and merchants, soldiers, clowns and drunkards, murderers, pimps, whores, fairies, monsters and pale, avenging ghosts 'strut and fret their hour upon the stage'. Murders and suicides abound; swords flash, blood flows, poison drips, and lovers sigh; yet there is always time for old men to talk of growing apples and for gardeners to discuss the weather.

In the four hundred years since they were written, they have become known and loved in every land; they are no longer the property of one country and one people, they are the priceless possession of the world.

His life, from what we know of it, was not astonishing. The stories that have attached themselves to him are remarkable only for their ordinariness: poaching deer, sleeping off a drinking bout under a wayside tree. There are no duels, no loud, passionate loves, no excesses of any kind. He was not one of your unruly geniuses whose habits are more interesting than their works. From all accounts, he was of a gentle, honourable disposition, a good businessman, and a careful father.

He was born on April 23rd 1564, to John and Mary Shakespeare of Henley Street, Stratford-upon-Avon. He was their third child and first son. When he was four or five he began his education at the local petty school. He left the local grammar school when he was about fourteen, in all probability to help in his father's glove-making shop. When he was eighteen, he married Anne Hathaway, who lived in a nearby village. By the time he was twenty-one, he was the father of three children, two daughters and a son.

Then, it seems, a restless mood came upon him. Maybe he travelled, maybe he was, as some say, a schoolmaster in the country; but at some time during the next seven years, he went to London and found employment in the theatre. When he was twenty-eight, he was already well enough known as an actor and playwright to excite the spiteful envy of a rival, who referred to him as 'an upstart crow'.

He mostly lived and worked in London until his mid-forties, when he returned to his family and home in Stratford, where he remained in prosperous circumstances until his death on April 23rd 1616, his fifty-second birthday.

He left behind him a widow, two daughters (his son died in childhood), and the richest imaginary world ever created by the human mind.

LEON GARFIELD

The list of the plays contained in the First Folio of 1623. This was the first collected edition of Shakespeare's plays and was gathered together by two of his fellow actors, John Hemmings and Henry Condell.

A CATALOGVE

of the feuerall Comedies, Histories, and Tragedies contained in this Volume.

The Theatre in Shakespeare's Day

IN 1989 AN ARCHAEOLOGICAL discovery was made on the south bank of the Thames that sent shivers of delight through the theatre world. A fragment of Shakespeare's own theatre, the Globe, where many of his plays were first performed, had been found.

This discovery has fuelled further interest in how Shakespeare himself conceived and staged his plays. We know a good deal already, and archaeology as well as documentary research will no doubt reveal more, but although we can only speculate on some of the details, we have a good idea of what the Elizabethan theatre-goer saw, heard and smelt when he went to see a play by William Shakespeare at the Globe.

It was an entirely different experience from anything we know today. Modern theatres have roofs to keep out the weather. If it rained on the Globe, forty per cent of the play-goers got wet. Audiences today sit on cushioned seats, and usually (especially if the play is by Shakespeare) watch and listen in respectful silence. In the Globe, the floor of the theatre was packed with a riotous crowd of garlic-reeking apprentices, house servants and artisans, who had each paid a penny to stand for the entire duration of the play, to buy nuts and apples from the food-sellers, to refresh themselves with bottled ale, relieve themselves, perhaps, into buckets by the back wall, to talk, cheer, catcall, clap and hiss if the play did not please them.

The Globe Theatre

In the galleries that rose in curved tiers around the inside of the building sat those who could afford to pay two pennies for a seat, and the benefits of a roof over their heads. Here, the middle ranking citizens, the merchants, the sea captains, the clerks from the Inns of Court, would sit crammed into their small eighteen inch space and look down upon the 'groundlings' below. In the 'Lords' room', the rich and the great, noblemen and women, courtiers and foreign ambassadors had to pay sixpence each for the relative comfort and luxury of their exclusive position directly above the stage, where they smoked tobacco, and overlooked the rest.

We are used to a stage behind an arch, with wings on either side, from which the actors come on and into which they disappear. In the Globe, the stage was a platform thrusting out into the middle of the floor, and the audience, standing in the central yard, surrounded it on three sides. There were no wings. Three doors at the back of the stage were used for all exits and entrances. These were sometimes covered by a curtain, which could be used as a prop.

The Workes of William Shakespeare,

containing all his Comedies, Histories, and
Tragedies : Truely set forth, according to their first
ORIGINALL.

The Names of the Principall Actors
in all these Playes.

William Shakespeare.

Richard Burbadge.

John Hemmings.

Augustine Phillips.

William Kempt.

Thomas Poope.

George Bryan.

Henry Condell.

William Slye.

Richard Cowly.

John Lowine.

Samuell Crosse.

Alexander Cooke.

Samuel Gilburne.

Robert Armin.

William Ostler.

Nathan Field.

John Underwood.

Nicholas Tooley.

William Ecclestone.

Joseph Taylor.

Robert Benfield.

Robert Goughe.

Richard Robinson.

Iohn Shancke.

Iohn Rice.

From this list of actors, we can see that William Shakespeare not only wrote plays but also acted in them. The Globe theatre, where these actors performed, is now being rebuilt close to its original site on the south bank of the river Thames.

Today we sit in a darkened theatre or cinema, and look at a brilliantly lit stage or screen, or we sit at home in a small, private world of our own, watching a luminous television screen. The close-packed, rowdy crowd at the Globe, where the play started at two o'clock in the afternoon, had no artificial light to enhance their illusion. It was the words that moved them. They came to listen, rather than to see.

No dimming lights announced the start of the play. A blast from a trumpet and three sharp knocks warned the audience that the action was about to begin. In the broad daylight, the actor could see the audience as clearly as the audience could see him. He spoke directly to the crowd, and held them with his eyes, following their reactions. He could play up to the raucous laughter that greeted the comical, bawdy scenes, and gauge the emotional response to the higher flights of poetry. Sometimes he even improvised speeches of his own. He was surrounded by, enfolded by, his audience.

The stage itself would seem uncompromisingly bare to our eyes. There was no scenery. No painted backdrops suggested a forest, or a castle, or the sumptuous interior of a palace. Shakespeare painted the scenery with his words, and the imagination of the audience did the rest.

Props were brought onto the stage only when they were essential for the action. A bed would be carried on when a character needed to lie on it. A throne would be let down from above when a king needed to sit on it. Torches and lanterns would suggest that it was dark, but the main burden of persuading an audience, at three o'clock in the afternoon, that it was in fact the middle of the night, fell upon the language.

In our day, costume designers create a concept as part of the production of a play into which each costume fits. Shakespeare's actors were responsible for their own costumes. They would use what was to hand in the 'tiring house' (dressing room), or supplement it out of their own pockets. Classical, medieval and Tudor clothes could easily appear side by side in the same play.

No women actors appeared on a public stage until many years after Shakespeare's death, for at that time it would have been considered shame-less. The parts of young girls were played by boys. The parts of older women were played by older men.

In 1613 the Globe theatre was set on fire by a spark from a cannon during a performance of Henry VIII, and it burnt to the ground. The actors, includ-ing Shakespeare himself, dug into their own pockets and paid for it to be rebuilt. The new theatre lasted until 1642, when it closed again. Now, in the 1990s, the Globe is set to rise again as a committed band of actors, scholars and enthusiasts are raising the money to rebuild Shakespeare's theatre in its original form a few yards from its previous site.

From the time when the first Globe theatre was built until today, Shakespeare's plays have been performed in a vast variety of languages, styles, costumes and techniques, on stage, on film, on television and in animated film. Shakespeare himself, working within the round wooden walls of his theatre, would have been astonished by it all.

PATRICK SPOTTISWOODE
Director of Education,
Globe Theatre Museum

SHAKESPEARE TODAY

SHAKESPEARE IS ALIVE TODAY! Although William Shakespeare the man lies long buried in Stratford-upon-Avon parish church, he lives on in countless millions of hearts and minds.

Imagine that cold April day in 1616. The small funeral procession labours slowly along Church Street. Huge black horses draw the wooden cart bearing the simple coffin. On the coffin, a few daffodils and primroses, plucked only minutes before from the garden of New Place, gravely nod with each jolt and jar of the rutted road.

Most of Stratford's citizens have turned out, muffled against the biting wind, to see the last appearance of their wealthy neighbour. You couldn't call it a crowd. Just small respectful groups clustering the dry places on the roadside, careful to avoid the mud splashed up by the great hooves of the lumbering horses.

Men and women briefly bow their heads as the dead man and the black-clad mourners pass. The townspeople share their opinions, as neighbours do. "He used to do some acting, didn't he?" "Made a lot of money in London. Writing plays, I think." "Used to come home once a year to see his family, but nobody here really knew a lot about Master Shakespeare." "Wasn't he a poet?" "Big landowner hereabouts anyway. All those fields over at Welcombe."

Past the Guild Chapel where he had worshipped as a boy. Past the school where long ago his imagination was fired by language. At the churchyard gate, under the sad elms, six men effortlessly heave the coffin on to their shoulders. William Shakespeare is about to enter his parish church for the last time.

Nobody at that long ago funeral guessed that they were saying goodbye to a man who would become the most famous Englishman of his age – perhaps of all time.

Shakespeare lives on. He weaves familiar themes into his tales: the conflicts between parents and children, love at first sight, the power struggles of war and politics. His language is heard everywhere. If you ever call someone 'a blinking idiot' or 'a tower of strength', or describe them as 'tongue-tied', or suffering from 'green-eyed jealousy', or being 'dead as a doornail', you are speaking the language of Shakespeare.

If you say 'it was Greek to me' or 'parting is such sweet sorrow', or that something is 'too much of a good thing' and that you 'have not slept one wink', the words of Shakespeare are alive in your mouth. Shakespeare's language has a power all of its own, rich in emotional intensity. Because he was a poet who wrote plays, he could make even the simplest words utterly memorable. All around the world people know Hamlet's line 'To be or not to be, that is the question.'

Shakespeare is still performed today because of the electrifying power of his storytelling. Whether his story is about love or murder, or kings and queens, he keeps you on the edge of your seat wanting to know what happens next.

He created well over nine hundred characters in his plays. However large or small the part, each character springs vividly to life in performance. They live in our imagination because they are so much like people today. They experience the same emotions that everyone feels and recognises: love, jealousy, fear, courage, ambition, pride … and a hundred others.

In every play, Shakespeare invites us to imagine what the characters are like, and for nearly four hundred years people have accepted Shakespeare's invitation. The plays have been re-imagined in very many ways. They have been shortened, added to, and set in very different periods of history. They have been translated into many languages and performed all over the world. Shakespeare lives because all persons in every age and every society can make their own interpretations and performances of Shakespeare.

The creators of *The Animated Tales* have re-imagined *The Taming of the Shrew* in a 26 minute animated film. You too can make your own living Shakespeare. Read the text that follows, and watch the video. Then try reading the play either by yourself, changing your voice to suit the different characters, or with friends, and record it on a tape recorder. If you have a toy theatre, try staging it with characters and scenery that you make and paint yourself. Or collect together a cast and create your own production for your family and friends.

Dr Rex Gibson

Dr Rex Gibson is the director of the Shakespeare and Schools Project which is part of the Institute of Education at the University of Cambridge.

In 1994 he was awarded the Sam Wanamaker International Shakespeare Award for his outstanding contribution to the world's knowledge of the works of Shakespeare.

What They Said of Him

One will ever find, in searching his works, new cause for astonishment and admiration.

GOETHE

Shakespeare was a writer of all others the most calculated to make his readers better as well as wiser.

SAMUEL TAYLOR COLERIDGE

An overstrained enthusiasm is more pardonable with respect to Shakespeare than the want of it; for our admiration cannot easily surpass his genius.

WILLIAM HAZLITT

It required three hundred years for England to begin to hear those two words that the whole world cries in her ear – William Shakespeare.

VICTOR HUGO

He has left nothing to be said about nothing or anything.

JOHN KEATS

The stream of time, which is continually washing the dissoluble fabrics of other poets, passes without injury by the adamant of Shakespeare.

SAMUEL JOHNSON

THE TAMING OF
THE SHREW

THE TAMING OF THE SHREW

Written, probably, in 1592, when the playwright was twenty-eight, *The Taming of the Shrew* is one of Shakespeare's earliest comedies. It is also one of his funniest. For four hundred years, the antics of Kate and Petruchio, as they trade insults, blows and kisses on their stormy way from courtship to marriage to perfect love and understanding, have filled the world's theatres with laughter and delight. But there is more to the play than a knockabout, boisterous battle of the sexes. It is a play about change, about transformation, about the magic of the theatre itself, when, at one moment, we are watching a group of people in strange costume strutting about on bare boards, and the next, we are in a street in sunny Padua, watching old Baptista Minola, trying to marry off his turbulent daughter Kate to whoever is brave enough to take her ...

THE CHARACTERS IN THE PLAY

in order of appearance

CHRISTOPHER SLY	*a tinker*
THE HOSTESS OF THE INN	
A LORD	
TWO SERVANTS	
BAPTISTA	*a rich citizen of Padua*
KATERINA	*his elder daughter*
BIANCA	*his younger daughter*
GREMIO	*a rich old citizen of Padua, suitor to Bianca*
HORTENSIO	*a gentleman of Padua, suitor to Bianca*
PETRUCHIO	*a gentleman of Verona, suitor to Katerina*
SERVANT	
GRUMIO	*servant to Petruchio*
LUCENTIO	*a gentleman of Pisa, suitor to Bianca*
NATHANIEL	*a servant*
PETER	*a servant*
TAILOR	
A RICH WIDOW	

The curtain rises on the outside of a country inn. Christopher Sly, the tinker, is drunk. Indeed, he is not often sober; and the hostess of the inn where he does his drinking has had enough of him.

HOSTESS'S VOICE   A pair of stocks, you rogue!

The door bursts open and out staggers Sly. He slides down the tethering post, and finishes up on the ground. He sleeps, his mouth wide open – a picture of drunken brutishness. There is a winding of horns. Enter a lord from hunting, with his train. He sees the recumbent Sly.

LORD   Grim death, how foul and loathsome is thy visage. (*Sly stirs, hiccups and snores.*)

SLY   The Slys are no rogues.

The lord starts back. He frowns, then smiles, as a thought strikes him. He beckons his servants about him.

LORD (*confidentially*) Sirs, I will practise on this drunken man.

The drunken Sly is transported to the lord's mansion where he is wrapped in new clothes, rings put upon his fingers, a banquet laid for him, and servants ordered to wait upon him as if he was indeed the lord of the mansion.

SLY (*waking*) For God's sake, a pot of small ale!

1ST SERVANT Your honour –

2ND SERVANT Your lordship –

SLY Call me not 'honour', nor 'lordship'. Am I not Christopher Sly, old Sly's son of Burton Heath?

LORD Thou art a lord and nothing but a lord.

2ND SERVANT These fifteen years you have been in a dream.

SLY These fifteen years! By my fay, a goodly nap! Upon my life, I am a lord indeed!

1ST SERVANT Your doctors thought it good you hear a play and frame your mind to mirth and merriment.

SLY   Well, we'll see it.

Sly is led from his bed to a great hall, at the farthest end of which is a curtained stage. The performance is about to begin.

The curtain rises on a street in Padua. Enter Baptista with his two daughters, Katerina and Bianca, together with Bianca's suitors, young Hortensio and old Gremio.

BAPTISTA   Gentlemen, importune me no farther for how I firmly am resolved you know – that is, not to bestow my youngest daughter before I have a husband for the elder. If either of you both love Katerina, leave shall you have to court her at your pleasure.

While her father speaks, Katerina – Kate – a wild and fearsome lass, is doing her best, by means of surreptitious pinches, kicks and tweakings of her fair plaits, to make her angel sister Bianca's life a misery.

GREMIO   To cart her rather! She's too rough for me!

KATE   (*to Baptista*) I pray you, sir, is it your will to make a stale of me amongst these mates?

HORTENSIO   'Mates', maid? No mates for you unless you were of gentler, milder mould. (*Kate threatens him with her fist. Hortensio backs away.*) From all such devils, good Lord deliver us!

GREMIO	(*skipping behind Hortensio*) And me too, good Lord!
BAPTISTA	Bianca, get you in. (*She looks downcast.*) And let it not displease thee, good Bianca, for I will love thee ne'er the less, my girl.
KATE	(*pulling Bianca's hair*) A pretty peat!
BIANCA	Sister, content you in my discontent. Sir, to your pleasure I humbly subscribe. (*She goes towards the door of her house, picking up a pretty guitar hung with ribbons and trailing it behind her.*)
GREMIO	Why, will you mew her up, Signor Baptista, for this fiend of hell?

As she dawdles, we see Lucentio, a young gallant, peering round a pillar at Bianca – obviously much attracted!

BAPTISTA	Gentlemen, content ye. I am resolved. (*Bianca goes into the house. Baptista follows, then pauses and turns to Kate.*) Katerina, you may stay. (*He goes in.*)
KATE	Why, and I trust I may go too, may I not? Ha!

She flounces into the house and slams the door violently. The gentlemen look at one another. Comes another loud bang as another door is slammed. They jump, and Lucentio does too.

It was a wretched state of affairs! No matter the suitors' sighs, old Baptista would never give his consent to the marriage of the fair Bianca until a husband was found for Katerina. And no consent, no dowry.

The scene changes to Petruchio, a gentleman from Verona, on horseback, knocking at Hortensio's window. Hortensio greets him enthusiastically.

HORTENSIO   My good friend Petruchio! What happy gale blows you to Padua here from old Verona?

PETRUCHIO   Such wind as scatters young men through the world. Signor Hortensio, I come to wive it wealthily in Padua; if weathily, then happily in Padua.

HORTENSIO   (*thoughtfully*) I can, Petruchio, help thee to a wife with wealth enough, and young, and beauteous, brought up as best becomes a gentlewoman. Her only fault – and that is faults enough – is that she is intolerable curst, and shrewd and froward. I would not wed her for a mine of gold!

PETRUCHIO   Hortensio, peace. Thou know'st not gold's effect. I will not sleep, Hortensio, till I see her . . .

Outside Baptista's house. Kate emerges, followed by a weeping Bianca, her hands tied.

BIANCA   Good sister, wrong me not, nor wrong yourself, to make a bondmaid and a slave of me.

Kate, detecting spite in the last remark, drags Bianca to the fountain. Baptista appears.

BAPTISTA   Why, how now dame, whence grows this insolence? Poor girl, she weeps. (*He unties her hands and turns to Kate.*) For shame, thou hilding of a devilish spirit, why dost thou wrong her that did ne'er wrong thee? Bianca, get thee in.

Bianca goes in.

KATE   Nay, now I see she is your treasure, she must have a husband, I must dance barefoot on her wedding day! Talk not to me, I will go sit and weep, till I can find occasion for revenge! (*She rushes into the house, with the inevitable slamming of the door.*)

BAPTISTA   Was ever gentleman thus grieved as I? But who comes here?

Enter Petruchio, who greets Baptista courteously.

PETRUCHIO   I am a gentleman of Verona, sir. Petruchio is my name. Pray have you not a daughter called Katerina, fair and virtuous?

BAPTISTA   I have a daughter, sir, called Katerina.

PETRUCHIO   Signor Baptista, my business asketh haste, and every day I cannot come to woo. Then tell me, if I get your daughter's love, what dowry shall I have with her to wife?

BAPTISTA   (*looking startled*) After my death the one half of my lands, and in possession twenty thousand crowns.

PETRUCHIO   (*nodding approvingly*) Let covenants be therefore drawn between us.

BAPTISTA   (*suddenly overcome with conscience*) Ay, where the special thing is well obtained, that is, her love; for that is all in all.

PETRUCHIO   Why, that is nothing; for I tell you, father, I am as peremptory as she proud-minded, and when two raging fires meet together they do consume the thing that feeds their fury.

BAPTISTA   Well mayst thou woo, and happy be thy speed! Be thou armed for some unhappy words. Shall I send my daughter Kate to you?

PETRUCHIO   I pray you do, I'll attend her here . . . (*Baptista, unable to believe his good fortune, hastens within. Petruchio is alone.*)

Kate appears. She eyes Petruchio curiously, as he does her. It is plain that an instant interest has been kindled between them, and they regard one another as worthy adversaries.

PETRUCHIO   Good morrow, Kate – for that's your name, I hear.

KATE   Well have you heard, but something hard of hearing; they call me Katherine that do talk of me.

PETRUCHIO   You lie, in faith, for you are called plain Kate, and bonny Kate, and sometimes Kate the curst. But Kate, the prettiest Kate in Christendom, hearing thy mildness praised in every town, thy virtues spoke of, and thy beauty sounded, myself am moved to woo thee for a wife!

KATE   'Moved', in good time! Let him that moved you hither remove you hence!

PETRUCHIO   Come, come, you wasp, i' faith, you are too angry.

KATE   If I be waspish, best beware my sting!

PETRUCHIO   My remedy then is to pluck it out!

KATE   Ay, if the fool could find it where it lies.

PETRUCHIO   Who knows not where a wasp does wear his sting? In his tail. (*He puts his hand on her bottom. She breaks loose.*)

KATE   And so farewell! (*She turns to go.*)

PETRUCHIO   Nay, come again. Good Kate, I am a gentleman –

KATE   That I'll try! (*She strikes him.*)

PETRUCHIO   I swear I'll cuff you if you strike again!

KATE   If you strike me you are no gentleman. (*They struggle.*)

PETRUCHIO   In sooth, you scape not so!

KATE   Let me go!

PETRUCHIO   (*releasing her so suddenly that she falls*) Why does the world report that Kate doth limp? O sland'rous world! Kate like the hazel twig is straight and slender. O let me see thee walk. Thou dost not halt.

KATE   Go, fool.

PETRUCHIO   Am I not wise?

KATE   Yes, keep you warm.

PETRUCHIO   Marry, so I mean, sweet Katherine, in thy bed. Now, Kate, I am a husband for your turn. For I am he am born to tame you, Kate, and bring you from a wild Kate to a Kate conformable as other household Kates.

It is apparent that Kate, in spite of herself, is much attracted to Petruchio, and his praise of her beauty does not go unnoticed. Old Baptista arrives.

BAPTISTA   Now, Signor Petruchio, how speed you with my daughter?

PETRUCHIO   How but well, sir? We have 'greed so well together that upon Sunday is the wedding day!

KATE   I'll see thee hanged on Sunday first.

Petruchio laughs, and confides to Baptista, unheard by Kate.

PETRUCHIO   'Tis bargained 'twixt us twain, being alone, that she shall still be curst in company. I tell you 'tis incredible to believe how much she loves me! O, the kindest Kate! She hung about my neck, and kiss on kiss she vied so fast, that in a twink she won me to her love!

BAPTISTA   I know not what to say, but give me your hands. God send you joy; Petruchio, 'tis a match.

PETRUCHIO   Provide the feast, father, and bid the guests: I will to Venice; Sunday comes apace. We will have rings, and things, and fine array. And kiss me, Kate, we will be married o' Sunday!

Kate glares at Petruchio, then at her father, then at Petruchio again. She kisses him; then, wiping the kiss off her lips, rushes into the house, slamming the door behind her. Baptista looks dismayed; but Petruchio wags a finger as if to say, 'I told you so', and departs. Baptista sighs with relief.

Invitations are dispatched and Kate's wedding-gown is prepared. By Sunday, the bride is ready, and everyone awaits the coming of the bridegroom. They wait, and they wait, and they wait.

KATE   I told you, I, he was a frantic fool. Now must the world point at poor Katherine and say, 'Lo, there is mad Petruchio's wife, if it would please him come and marry her!' (*She rushes out weeping in fury and a sense of betrayal.*)

BAPTISTA   Go, girl, I cannot blame thee now to weep, for such an injury would vex a saint.

A servant enters, breathless.

SERVANT   Master, master, news, and such news as you never heard of!

BAPTISTA   Is he come?

For answer, the servant points, and Petruchio, accompanied by his servant, appears. He is dressed in 'a new hat and an old jerkin; a pair of old breeches thrice turned; a pair of boots that have been candle-cases, one buckled, another laced; an old rusty sword . . .' In short, a very scarecrow. He dismounts. The guests watch, amazed.

PETRUCHIO   (*ignoring the stares*) Where is Kate? The morning wears, 'tis time we were in church.

BAPTISTA   But thus I trust you will not marry her.

PETRUCHIO   Good sooth, even thus. To me she's married, not unto my clothes. But what a fool am I to chat with you, when I should bid good morrow to my bride, and seal the title with a lovely kiss! (*He departs.*)

All stare at one another appalled.

In Baptista's house, the wedding guests await the arrival of the happy couple. Petruchio enters with his tousled bride.

PETRUCHIO   Gentlemen and friends, I thank you for your pains. I know you think to dine with me today, but so it is, my haste doth call me hence.

BAPTISTA   Is't possible you will away tonight?

PETRUCHIO   I must away before night come.

GREMIO   Let me entreat you to stay 'til after dinner.

PETRUCHIO   It cannot be.

KATE   Let me entreat you. Now if you love me, stay.

PETRUCHIO   Grumio, my horse!

KATE   Nay then, do what thou canst, I will not go today, no, nor tomorrow, not till I please myself. Gentlemen, forward to the bridal dinner. I see a woman may be made a fool if she had not a spirit to resist.

PETRUCHIO   They shall go forward, Kate, at thy command. – Obey the bride, you that attend on her. Go to the feast, and carouse full measure to her maidenhead. But for my bonny Kate, she must with me. I will be master of what is mine own.

Kate shows every sign of defiance and seeks support from her father and the guests. It is not forthcoming. At length, Petruchio seizes her about the waist, and, with fiercely drawn sword, rushes away with her, followed by his servant, Grumio. The guests crowd after them.

Outside, Kate, Petruchio and Grumio gallop away on three horses. Inside, all is cheerfulness. Bianca is queening it among her admirers.

LUCENTIO   Mistress, what is your opinion of your sister?

BIANCA   That being mad herself, she's madly mated!

The three riders in a wet and windy landscape. Kate's horse stumbles and she tumbles down. The horse bolts. Petruchio hoists Kate up onto his own horse, and away they ride, he behind, she in front, muddy and furious.

At last, they arrive at Petruchio's house in Verona where the servants are making ready for the arrival of the master and his bride.

PETRUCHIO   Where be these knaves? What, no man at door to hold my stirrup nor to take my horse?

ALL SERVANTS   Here sir, here sir, here sir!

PETRUCHIO   Go, rascals, go and fetch my supper in! (*He sings.*)
'Where is the life that late I led?' Be merry, Kate!
Some water here! What ho! (*Water is brought.*)
Come, Kate, and wash and welcome heartily! (*He stretches out his foot and trips the servant.*) You whoreson villain, will you let it fall? (*He threatens the man.*)

KATE   Patience, I pray you, 'twas a fault unwilling.

Food is set out on a table.

PETRUCHIO   A whoreson, beetle-headed, flap-eared knave! Come, Kate, sit down, I know you have a stomach. (*Kate sits.*) What's this? Mutton?

SERVANT   Ay.

PETRUCHIO   'Tis burnt, and so is all the meat! How durst you villains serve it thus to me?

Petruchio hurls the dishes at the servants, who scatter in terror.

KATE   I pray you, husband, be not so disquiet. The meat was well –

PETRUCHIO   I tell thee, Kate, 'twas burnt and dried away, and I am expressly forbid to touch it, for it engenders choler, planteth anger – and better 'twere that both of us did fast! Come, I will bring thee to thy bridal chamber.

He pulls the hungry Kate away from the table, and away to their bedroom. The servants begin to clear away the wreckage of the meal.

NATHANIEL   Peter, didst ever see the like?

PETER   He kills her in her own humour.

The servants depart. A moment later, Petruchio appears, very furtively. He peers about him, then, hastily, retrieves whatever food is left, and gobbles it down hungrily. As he munches and swallows, he confides:

PETRUCHIO   Thus have I politicly begun my reign. Last night she slept not, nor tonight she shall not. He that knows better how to tame a shrew, now let him speak . . .

While Kate is learning one lesson, her sister, the fair Bianca, is learning another . . .

In Baptista's house, Bianca is closeted with her new suitor, Lucentio, a rich young man from Pisa, who cunningly disguised as a schoolmaster has outbid his rivals and won Bianca's heart.

BIANCA   What, master, read you?

LUCENTIO   The Art to Love.

BIANCA   And may you prove, sir, master of your art!

LUCENTIO   While you, sweet dear, prove mistress of my heart.

He removes his whiskers and kisses her. Meanwhile, Hortensio and Gremio give up their hopes for Bianca's love: Gremio retires to his moneybags, and Hortensio decides to marry a rich widow. But first he calls at his friend Petruchio's house.

He finds Kate seated at a table. Petruchio and Hortensio enter with a dish of meat.

HORTENSIO   Mistress, what cheer?

KATE   Faith, as cold as can be.

PETRUCHIO   Pluck up thy spirits! Here, love, thou seest how diligent I am to dress thy meat myself. What, not a word? Nay then, thou lov'st it not. Here, take away this dish.

A servant comes forward.

KATE   I pray you let it stand.

PETRUCHIO   The poorest service is repaid with thanks, and so shall mine before you touch the meat.

KATE   I thank you, sir.

PETRUCHIO   Kate, eat apace. And now, my honey love, we will return unto thy father's house, and revel it as bravely as the best, with silken coats and caps, and golden rings – what, hast thou dined? (*He takes away her unfinished plate.*) The tailor stays thy leisure.

The tailor enters.

TAILOR   Here is the cap your worship did bespeak.

PETRUCHIO   Why, 'tis a cockle or a walnut shell. A baby's cap. Come, let me
              have a bigger.

KATE   I'll have no bigger. Gentlewomen wear such caps as these.

PETRUCHIO   When you are gentle, you shall have one too, and not till then.

HORTENSIO   That will not be in haste!

PETRUCHIO   Thy gown? Come, tailor, let us see it. (*The tailor displays the
              gown.*) What's this? A sleeve? Carved like an apple tart? Here's
              snip and nip, and cut and slish and slash! (*The tailor retreats,
              baffled.*)

HORTENSIO   (*aside*) I see she's like to have neither cap nor gown.

PETRUCHIO   I'll none of it! (*To the tailor*) Away, thou rag, thou quantity,
              thou remnant! (*He rips the dress. Kate is in despair.*)

KATE   I never saw a better-fashioned gown.

Petruchio mutters to Hortensio as tailor retreats.

PETRUCHIO   Hortensio, say thou wilt see the tailor paid. Well, come my
              Kate, we will unto your father's, even in these honest mean
              habiliments. Our purses shall be proud, our garments poor, for
              'tis the mind that makes the body rich. Let's see, I think 'tis
              now some seven o'clock, and well we may come there by
              dinner-time.

KATE   I dare assure you, sir, 'tis almost two.

PETRUCHIO   It shall be what o'clock I say it is.

HORTENSIO   (*aside*) Why, so this gallant will command the sun!

*The scene changes to Petruchio, Kate and Hortensio on
horseback.*

PETRUCHIO   Come on, a God's name, once more towards our father's.
              Good Lord, how bright and goodly shines the moon!

KATE The moon? The sun! It is not moonlight now.

PETRUCHIO I say it is the moon that shines so bright.

KATE I know it is the sun that shines so bright.

PETRUCHIO (*stopping*) Evermore crossed and crossed, nothing but crossed.

KATE Forward, I pray, and be it moon or sun, or what you please –

PETRUCHIO I say it is the moon.

KATE I know it is the moon.

PETRUCHIO Nay, then you lie. It is the blessed sun.

KATE Then God be blessed, it is the blessed sun, but sun it is not, when you say it is not, and the moon changes even as your mind; what you shall have it named, even that it is, and so it shall be so for Katherine.

And so they come to Padua. Hortensio marries his rich widow, and Bianca marries her lover Lucentio. And afterwards, there is a great banquet.

BAPTISTA   (*becoming maudlin*) Now, in good sadness, son Petruchio, I think thou hast the veriest shrew of all.

PETRUCHIO   Well, I say no. And therefore, for assurance, let's each one send unto his wife, and he whose wife is most obedient, shall win the wager which we will propose.

HORTENSIO   Content. What's the wager?

LUCENTIO   Twenty crowns.

PETRUCHIO	Twenty crowns? I'll venture so much of my hawk or hound, but twenty times so much upon my wife!
LUCENTIO	A hundred then.
PETRUCHIO	A match! 'Tis done.
HORTENSIO	Who shall begin?
LUCENTIO	That will I. (*To servant*) Go, bid your mistress come to me.

The servant leaves, watched contentedly by Lucentio and Baptista. Soon he returns.

LUCENTIO	How now, what news?
SERVANT	Sir, my mistress sends you word that she is busy, and she cannot come.
PETRUCHIO	How? 'She's busy, and she cannot come'? Is that an answer?
GREMIO	Pray God, sir, your wife send you not a worse!
HORTENSIO	(*to servant*) Go and entreat my wife to come to me forthwith. (*The servant leaves the room.*)
PETRUCHIO	O ho, entreat her! Nay, then she needs must come!
HORTENSIO	I am afraid, sir, do what you can, yours will not be entreated. (*The servant returns.*) Now, where's my wife?
SERVANT	She will not come; she bids you come to her.

PETRUCHIO   Worse and worse; 'She will not come'! O vile, intolerable, not to be endured. (*To Grumio, his servant*) Go to your mistress, say I command her to come to me. (*Grumio departs.*)

HORTENSIO   I know her answer.

PETRUCHIO   What?

HORTENSIO   She will not.

Kate enters charmingly.

KATE   What is your will, sir, that you send for me?

PETRUCHIO   Where is your sister, and Hortensio's wife?

KATE   They sit conferring by the parlour fire.

PETRUCHIO   Away, I say, and bring them hither straight!

Kate leaves.

LUCENTIO   Here is a wonder, if you talk of wonder!

HORTENSIO   And so it is. I wonder what it bodes.

PETRUCHIO   Marry, peace it bodes, and love, and quiet life.

BAPTISTA   Now fair befall thee, good Petruchio! The wager thou hast won, and I will add unto their losses twenty thousand crowns, another dowry to another daughter, for she is changed, as she had never been!

PETRUCHIO   Nay, I will win my wager better yet. (*Kate enters, propelling the unwilling Bianca, now a grim and furious angel, and the widow.*) Katherine, that cap of yours becomes you not. Off with that bauble! (*Kate smiles, takes off the cap and treads on it.*)

WIDOW   Lord, let me never have cause to sigh till I be brought to such a silly pass!

BIANCA   Fie, what a foolish duty call you this?

LUCENTIO   I wish your duty were as foolish too! The wisdom of your duty, fair Bianca, hath cost me a hundred crowns since supper-time.

BIANCA   The more fool you for laying on my duty!

PETRUCHIO   Katherine, I charge thee tell these headstrong women what duty they do owe their lords and husbands.

WIDOW   She shall not!

KATE   (*with exaggeration, Petruchio finding it hard to restrain himself from laughing at their mutual joke*) Fie, fie, unknit that threatening unkind brow. It blots thy beauty. A woman moved is like a fountain troubled, muddy, ill-seeming, thick, bereft of beauty. Thy husband is thy lord, thy life, thy keeper – one that cares for thee; and for thy maintenance, commits his body to painful labour both by sea and land, whilst thou liest warm at home, secure and safe, and craves no other tribute at thy hands but love, fair looks, and true obedience – too little payment for so great a debt.

Kate lays her hands under her husband's feet with a dramatic flourish and smiles triumphantly up at him. He looks adoringly at her.

PETRUCHIO   Why, there's a wench! Come on, and kiss me, Kate! (*She does so. He turns to Lucentio.*) 'Twas I won the wager, and being a winner, God give you good night! (*They leave together, fondly entwined.*)

The play is over and Christopher Sly is fast asleep. The lord and his companions smile. The tinker's dream must end where it began.
    Sly is carried back to the ale-house where he had been found and left propped against the tethering-post. He awakes.

SLY   Sim, gi's some more wine. What's all the players gone? (*He surveys his own wretched attire, and sadly shakes his head.*) Am I not a lord? (*He sighs, then he smiles.*) I have had the bravest dream. I know now how to tame a shrew.

He rises uncertainly, and totters into the ale-house with some determination. A moment latter, he comes out, a good deal more rapidly than he went in, followed by a hail of household utensils.

HOSTESS'S VOICE   A pair of stocks, you rogue!

The curtain falls.

The Taming Of The Shrew

The Play, the Animated Video, the Author, and his Times

Study assignments by Linda Marsh, English Department, North Westminster Community School, London

It's hard to put ourselves in the position of Kate and Petruchio in *The Taming of the Shrew*; the world has come a long way since playwrights could joke about putting women in their place and get away with it. It's also difficult to discover from the ending what Shakespeare thought about how women and men in love should behave. As ever, his genius lies in presenting situations without forcing us to reach conclusions. These two lovers may, or may not, have come to love each other equally. Certainly we can turn to other plays by Shakespeare and find women like Beatrice in *Much Ado About Nothing* who says she will not marry 'till God make men of some other mettle than earth. Would it not grieve a woman to be overmastered with a piece of valiant dust? To make an account of her life to a clod of wayward marl?' And there is Juliet, whose love for Romeo is not concerned with battles over strength; she simply dies for love of him, and he for her.

We won't find one view of love in Shakespeare's plays, and there isn't one here, however tempting it is to think we glimpse it in Kate's final speech. There is a mystery at the heart of her marriage to Petruchio. When they walk off laughing, at the end, we are left to ponder their victories and defeats... were they quite what they seemed?

So although written for a particular kind of theatre and for the London audiences of the late sixteenth and early seventeenth century, Shakespeare's *The Taming of the Shrew* is for all times, and can be enjoyed in many different media: sound recordings, films, books or different kinds of productions in different kinds of theatres. The television series on which this book is based is a new approach: animations devised by Russian artists, spoken by a British cast of actors, and using Shakespeare's actual words in a specially prepared version.

The following assignments have been planned for you to use with your teacher to help you think more about the play. They include work on:

• its story, its characters, and the language they speak;
• the ideas and themes from *The Taming of the Shrew* and their connection with many aspects of life today;
• the artistic approach to the play in sixteenth and seventeenth-century England, in other productions at other times, and in this animated version.

Some of the assignments ask you to re-read the text or to research. Others invite you to act, and others to write. All of them ask you to think about the play - its words and ideas. Some you will be able to carry out only with the help of your teacher, but others you can do at school or home after watching the programmes or video and reading the script. The assignments are grouped into sections according to the aspect of the play being considered, but obviously your teacher will not wish you simply to work through them in order, and each of you can create your own study pattern from the range of assignments.

I hope that these assignments will help you to understand and enjoy the animated version of *The Taming of the Shrew* better, to re-read the text with greater enjoyment, and to learn more about Shakespeare and his theatre.

L.M.

The Study Assignments

1 *'Upon my life, I am a lord indeed!'*   SLY

When Sly wakes up, it seems too good to be true. His old clothes and hungry stomach are things of the past.

1.a What would be your 'dream come true'? Imagine you have just woken up to find everything has changed. Where are you? Who are you? Write it down.

2 *Baptista states the problem clearly and immediately. He has*   THE BEGINNING
two daughters, and convention dictates that the elder daughter should marry before the younger. But according to Gremio, Kate, the elder daughter, is a 'fiend from hell', so who will marry her? What does this mean for Bianca?

In the scene which follows, we get a good idea of what appropriate female behaviour is meant to be from watching Bianca and from listening to the criticism flying about.

2.a If you were Hortensio or Gremio, what would you be looking for? Describe your ideal woman.

2.b Kate's behaviour is a problem. Is this because it isn't seen to be civilised, or is it because she's female? In small groups, read the first scene through and then discuss it. It may help you to know the meaning of the following words:

'cart' - a whipping at the cart's tail was a punishment for prostitutes

'stale' - this could be a decoy or a prostitute

'mate' - partner, in this case, prospective partners for Kate

'mew' - confine. (A hawk would be put in a 'mew' at moulting time.)

2.c In pairs, rewrite the scene (of about nine or ten lines) where you demonstrate that one of the men is behaving problematically. You could use the same incidents as Shakespeare or quite different ones, according to your perception of how similar or different such male behaviour might be.

BIANCA

3 *Bianca's behaviour and Lucentio's courtship of her are in marked contrast to Petruchio's courtship of Kate. Do you see Bianca as truly pleasant or as someone who is 'too good to be true'? She certainly angers Kate. For whom do you have the most sympathy?*

3.a Imagine the two sisters in Bianca's bedroom after the scene in which she has been told to go inside and Kate has flounced in after her. In pairs, write down what you think they say to each other, then read it aloud to see how it sounds.

A SENSE OF ORDER

4 *Men in Shakespeare's time were encouraged to think of themselves as the head of their household. Women were supposed to look up to the men as their masters, and the children in turn took their place beneath their parents. Petruchio was not unusual in thinking of his position in this way. When he says, 'For I am he am born to tame you, Kate', he means not only that this is his special calling, but that as a man, the idea has tickled his fancy and he is exerting his natural right to claim her if he wants to.*

This was in keeping with a picture of the whole world as educated people saw it. God had created a 'Chain of Being', in which everything and every living creature was assigned a place. There was:

- *the mere existence of the inanimate class of the elements, liquids and metals. (But, for example, water is nobler than earth, the ruby more noble than topaz, gold over brass, etc.)*
- *the existence and life of the vegetative class (where, for example, the oak is nobler than the bramble).*
- *the existence, life and feeling of the sensitive class, including creatures such as shellfish which experience touch but not hearing, memory, or movement, moving up to animals with all these faculties, such as dogs and horses.*
- *the existence, life, feeling and understanding of man and the angels.*

But as elements nourish plants, and plants feed animals, and animals are eaten by man, so this is all part of man moving upwards towards God.

4.a Check whether you have understood this chain by seeing what you can add to the examples in each of the categories.

5 *Man's position in this 'Chain of Being' was obviously of most interest to those who thought about it. (The educated people were in a good position to decide what was right and wrong for everyone else.) Man was considered to have the possibilities within himself of being like the angels or the beasts. So much had been given to him: 'He passeth over the vast seas; he rangeth about the wide heavens by his contemplation and conceives the motions and the magnitudes of the stars... He is learned in every science... He talketh with angels yea with God himself. He hath all the creatures within his dominion.'*

This is how Shakespeare put it in Act II Sc. II of his play Hamlet:

'What a piece of work is a man! how noble in reason! how infinite in faculty! in form and moving how express and admirable! in action how like an angel! in apprehension how like a god! the beauty of the world! the paragon of animals!'

It was felt that families should be run as countries were, with someone at the head of each one. If families were well-ordered, then the country would be strong and prosper. Therefore men were supposed to exert their authority and women submit to it.

5.a The scene in *The Taming of the Shrew* in which the three husbands bet on who possesses the most obedient wife symbolizes their sense of importance as men and husbands. As a director of this scene on stage, how would you want to guide the actors through it so that this point gets across to the audience? If they are sitting down, would you want them to sit back with their legs crossed, casually twirling a glass? If they are standing, would one be leaning nonchalantly against a pillar?

Picture the scene and write down your stage directions for each of them. Include ideas for what the others could be doing while they are not speaking. Work from 'Now in good sadness' (page 42), to 'Go bid my mistress come to me' (page 43).

6 *There was a Gloucestershire saying:*

'A woman, a spaniel, and a walnut tree,
The more they are beaten, better they be.'

Men who laughed along with that would have had their joke confirmed in church. From 1562, the 'Homily on Marriage' (the eighteenth of many from which the parsons were ordered to read in church every Sunday) left congregations in no doubt about the inferior status, rights, and character of a wife. 'The woman is a weak creature...', probably best not beaten but definitely better off kept under control.

Legally, in marriage, the husband and wife became one person - and that person was the husband. He acquired absolute control of his wife's property and could sell it at will. One manuscript shows us that William Jeffes of Walton 'may have, possesse and enjoye all the goodes, chattels, household stuff, money and plate... landes, tenemented pastures, meadowes, groundes, commons and commodities whatsoever' that his wife-to-be, the widow Elinor, has. Another man, Will Shaftoe, decreed in his will of 1599, 'To my daughter Margery, 60 sheep and I bestow her in marriage upon Edward, son of Reynold Shaftoe of Thockerington.' She could, therefore, also be property.

6.a What evidence is there in the play that everyone understands the need to 'root romantic love in the rich soil of finance'? Copy out any of the lines you find spoken by the characters, and any information that may be contained in the narration or stage directions, that show us that men expected to get goods and money along with a wife.

6.b In the light of this, Baptista says something unexpected. What is it, and what does it say about him?

7 *Women were not the only ones to suffer oppression in many households of the times. While some families lived together in a loving and friendly way, it was generally held to be right to correct children in ways that would seem hard to us today. Many were terribly beaten as a matter of course. One man recalls, 'usually in my dreams I methought I saw my father always grievously angry with me.' And what about this? 'Cherishing marreth sons, but it utterly destroyeth daughters.'*

7.a This is a very different kind of world. How do you think you would have fitted into it? As a child living then, you would have had to accept most of what came your way. Imagine that you are a child or a teenager travelling back in time. You find yourself in an Elizabethan family with its tenderness held back by discipline, and a strong sense of the natural order of things. How might you feel? What might you do? How, as a boy or a girl, do you find yourself expected to behave? Take a look at some history books in your school or local library, then write a short story.

8 *It has been discovered that different threads of the story of* The Taming of the Shrew *have been found in old folk-tales recorded in France, Italy, Finland, Estonia, Lithuania, Sweden, Denmark, Iceland, Scotland, Ireland, Spain, Holland, Germany, the United States, India and Spanish America. It has also been staged in various forms, too, in this country to the present day. Different generations have changed different aspects of the story to reflect their own ideas. But clearly this is a story, whose essential features have had a strong appeal.*

THE STORY'S APPEAL

Here are two interesting examples of changes made in English theatres in 1668 and 1754:

• *John Lacey wrote 'Sauney the Scott: Or, The Taming of the Shrew' to include much more brutality. Petruchio thinks Kate is silent because she has toothache and sends for the barber to perform an extraction (a horrible operation) but she forces him off. He then says her silence means she's dead and is about to have her buried. Unsurprisingly she surrenders - without any of the grace, humour and dignity of Shakespeare's Kate.*

• *Garrick's 'Catherine and Petruchio' has the couple joining for the speech at the end in a friendly, comic ending to the marriage problems, Petruchio saying some of the speech himself.*

8.a Look at this line of Petruchio's from Shakespeare's script (see page 46):

'Why, there's a wench! Come on, and kiss me, Kate.'

Shakespeare often gives his actors lines that could be said in many different ways. This is part of his genius because it gives actors the opportunity to interpret the script in their own way. Garrick's cutting and staging of Kate's speech can only have one meaning. How differently can you read the line above to illuminate the understanding that Kate and Petruchio may have reached? For example, he could turn to the others or to the audience with a boastful swagger. How else could he react?

9 *Shakespeare is famous for his language. He brought a very wide range of different kinds of words together, often drawing on ordinary people's ways of putting things, but also on the*

LANGUAGE

learned patterns originating in Latin and Greek. He was able to express himself in a way that no one had thought of before, and created phrases that will remain in our language for ever because of his use of comparisons with very down-to-earth or powerful pictures.

These comparisons are called 'images' and a writer's use of them 'imagery'. There is an example in Petruchio's scheme to trick Kate when he says he'll tell her 'she sings as sweetly as a nightingale. Say that she frown, I'll say she looks as clear as morning roses, newly washed with dew.' On another occasion he likens them both to two raging fires, meeting together to burn each other up in their heat and intensity. The third image is of the wasp: Kate says, 'If I be waspish, best beware my sting!' Petruchio replies, 'My remedy then is to pluck it out!'

The most potent image of all expresses the threat to male authority that Kate's behaviour most profoundly stirs up. It is worse than shrewishness, it is a link with witchcraft itself. It suggests she has more powers than they can dream of, and while they joke, they shiver with uncertainty...

9.a Work with a partner to find this image. It is repeated three times in different ways in the first few pages of the script.

9.b To understand the full force of this image, look in the history books in your library for more information. The scold's bridle and the ducking stool were the people's way of combating their fears, and accusations of witchcraft took these fears further. The wealth of Kate's family, and her father's protection, kept her safe. Poor women would have been far less lucky.

10 *Plays written at this time were mostly written in a patterned form of poetry called 'blank verse'. This was developed amongst the actors and writers to enable them to move from the most ordinary lines of action to the highest moments of special feeling. Shakespeare undoubtedly developed this style of writing to its highest form. It had a regular rhythm of ten syllables to a line, stressed following unstressed. There were no rhymes, but the stress of the line was often used to give emphasis and bring out the special meaning.*

As you listen, it often sounds like the ordinary speech of prose - but when needed it can rise to unusually moving and powerful phrases. Here's an example from Act III Sc. II (printed in verse layout, not as in the script earlier in this book).

'To me she's married, not unto my clothes...
But what a fool am I, to chat with you,
When I should bid good-morrow to my bride,
And seal the title with a lovely kiss!'

Each line has ten beats and when you read it aloud you stress the even syllables. Try it.

To ME she's MARRied, NOT unTO my CLOTHES.

*This is called an '**Iambic Pentameter**'. 'Iambic' is the technical term for a pair of syllables in which the first is weak and the second stressed (e.g. 'today') and 'pent-' means 'five' as in 'pentagon'. There are five weak-strong pairs in the line. In the script version printed in this book, the lines have not been printed in that way because it is a slimmed-down version. Here, though, are two lines from one of the key speeches (in this book on page 29) printed to show the blank verse as it would have been in Shakespeare's day.*

'Thou must be married to no man but me.
For I am he am born to tame you, Kate...'

10.a Try reading that speech aloud. Can you hear the weak-strong pattern? The last syllable of each line gains a slightly stronger stress. In this way Shakespeare influences the emphasis and expression of the actor.

10.b Search through the script with a partner to see if you can find two more examples of blank verse.

11 *It can be interesting to see how other poets treat the theme of women and love. Here is Alfred, Lord Tennyson, the Victorian Poet Laureate (1809-1892):*

For him she plays, to him she sings
Of early faith and plighted vows:
She knows but matters of the house,
And he, he knows a thousand things.

Her faith is fixt and cannot move,
She darkly feels him great and wise,
She dwells on him with faithful eyes,
'I cannot understand: I love.'

This next excerpt is from 'For Colored Girls Who Have Considered Suicide When the Rainbow is Enuf' by Ntozake Shange (Methuen 1978).

lady in blue

one thing i dont need
is any more apologies
i got sorry greetin me at my front door
you can keep yrs
i dont know what to do wit em
they dont open doors
or bring the sun back
they dont make me happy
or get a mornin paper
didnt nobody stop usin my tears to wash cars
cuz a sorry

i am simply tired
of collectin
  i didnt know
  i was so important toyou
i'm gonna haveta throw some away
i cant get to the clothes in my closet
for alla the sorries
i'm gonna tack a sign to my door
leave a message by the phone
  'if you called
  to say yr sorry
  call somebody
  else
  i dont use em anymore'
i let sorry/ didnt meanta/ & how cd i know abt that
take a walk down a dark & musty street in brooklyn
i'm gonna do exactly what i want to
& i wont be sorry for none of it
letta sorry soothe yr soul/ i'm gonna soothe mine

you were always inconsistent
doin somethin & then bein sorry
beatin my heart to death
talkin bout you sorry

well
i will not call
i'm not goin to be nice
i will raise my voice
& scream & holler
& break things & race the engine
& tell all yr secrets bout yrself to yr face
& i will list in detail everyone of my wonderful lovers
& their ways
i will play oliver lake
loud
& i wont be sorry for none of it

i loved you on purpose
i was open on purpose
i still crave vulnerability & close talk
& i'm not even sorry bout you bein sorry
you can carry all the guilt & grime ya wanna
just dont give it to me
i cant use another sorry
next time
you should admit
you're mean/ low-down/ triflin/ & no count straight out
steada bein sorry alla the time
enjoy bein yrself

11.a These two pictures of women's lives are very different. One speaks of centuries of women looking up to their men. It is what Petruchio and his friends assume they are entitled to. The other speaks to women whose experience is more often of pain than of love, and it suggests a different kind of reality.

One is structured in verses with a rhyming pattern. The other has neither of these qualities but is a form of patterned prose, rising out of the woman's feelings as they surface.

How do the two structures form part of the message of these poems?

11.b What does Petruchio want from Kate? What does Kate want from him? If they were allowed breathing space away from the others, what might they have said to one another after a while? Write it down. You could use ordinary speech, a form of verse like Tennyson, or the kind of style that Ntozake Shange uses.

11.c Shakespeare's use of blank verse, popular in his day, contrasts with his use of prose for ordinary and conversational scenes in his plays. He uses verse when he wants to catch our particular attention. In the scene in which Petruchio and Kate look at the sun, and Kate is pressured to say it is the moon if he wants it to be, he uses verse to elevate this moment: it is an important one, because this is when she gives in. But does she do so with calmness? With wretchedness? Eagerness? Grace? Her tone is important in deciding whether she is giving up, humouring him, speaking in a flash of love, or whatever... How would *you* like her to say it? Work out with a partner how differently her words can be made to sound.

SUSPENSE

12 *There is a moment of huge suspense towards the end of the play, when the men have ordered their wives to appear and two have not. Will Kate come?*

12.a If you were directing the play and wanted to excite the audience, how would you ask Petruchio to act his part as he and Hortensio speak these lines (see page 44)?

Petruchio: (*to Gremio*) Go to your mistress, say I command her to come to me.

Hortensio: I know her answer.

Petruchio: What?

Hortensio: She will not.

THE ENDING

13 *What do you think Shakespeare wants us to read into Kate's final speech? She has some very definite things to say. They could be spoken seriously as if a lesson has been learnt. But they could be spoken wittily as if sharing a joke. Beaumont and Fletcher's play 'The Women's Prize: Or The Tamer Tam'd' reprimands the husband in a kind of answer to Shakespeare's play:*

> *They should not reign as Tyrants o'er their wives*
> *Nor can the women from this president*
> *Insult, or triumph; it being aptly meant,*
> *To teach both Sexes due equality;*
> *And as they stand bound, to love mutually.*

Sinead Cusack as Katherine and Alun Armstrong as Petruchio (RSC 1982)

13.a If Kate means to laugh with her husband, as if they are joining together against the others, it suggests that Petruchio has calmed down a bit too. You can't share a joke with someone whose sense of self-importance eclipses everything (unless, of course, the joke is seen as going his way!). What do you think of this interpretation? Could you argue that Petruchio has learnt lessons too? Discuss this with a partner.

13.b Kate undeniably says on page 46, 'Thy husband is thy lord, thy life, thy keeper - one that cares for thee; and for thy maintenance, commits his body to painful labour both by sea and land, whilst thou liest warm at home, secure and safe...'

Some women would wish to argue that there is great freedom for women in this situation. It isn't all about oppression and denial. What do you think about this?

13.c All the action takes place in a play within a play. Shakespeare has taken two steps away from reality. Perhaps all the while Kate has been in charge of her own fate, and wrought her own changes through falling in love; a very different fate from being bred as a bride with no other option. The drama could thus be seen as a double trick for the men in the audience. They think they are seeing one kind of drama, but the joke is on them. Is it?

COMEDY

14 *In Shakespeare's comedies there are both solemn and comic moments.* The Taming of the Shrew *is a play about a marriage and it is connected to his other comedies in which love grows and flowers despite obstacles. Over the years it has been played for laughs as well as reaching out to touch the hearts of audiences. There are boisterous scenes that can be very funny but there are also moments when 'man lays down his arms' and surrenders to the power and grace, the romance and the spirit that his heroine embodies. These points in the play can be unexpected, and it is the mark of the ambitious and successful director that she or he can continually surprise us.*

14.a In pairs, look at the scenes in which you could clearly aim to make your audience laugh. Now pose for a photograph, to capture the essence of one or two of the speeches here. What exactly is happening should be clear from the way you are standing and looking at or away from each other. See if the rest of the class can guess which point you've chosen.

14.b Now do the same but try to achieve the opposite effect.

14.c Some productions miss out the beginning and ending which is all about Sly and his dream. It can be fun and challenging to decide for yourself where and how you would like to begin to draw your audience in, and where you would choose to end the play. Your decisions depend on how you see *The Taming of the Shrew* and what you think the play is really about.

What would your decisions be? Discuss your ideas with your partner and then present them to the rest of the class.